T0146739

Contents

In the beginning, God created
the heavens and the earth.
Genesis 1:1 (ESV)

God provided

God provided
the way
for
our
sin
to be
forgiven,
enabling
us
to commune
with Him
on earth
and
in heaven.

REFLECTION ON GENESIS 6:5-8 (ESV)

In His heart God grieved

In His heart God grieved,
seeing evil
in the hearts of men.
"But Noah found favor
in the eyes of the LORD."
So, when the rains came,
the waters lifted up
a refuge built of trees,
and Noah and his family
rose above mountains
as the ark floated
on earth's cleansing seas.

REFLECTION ON GENESIS 22:1-14 (ESV)

"Here I am"

"Here I am,"
said Abraham,
and God told him
to sacrifice
his only son,
at which Abraham
did not protest or falter,
knowing the Lord
will provide
when a man
binds his heart
and lays it on the altar.

Fruitful in the land of his tears

Fruitful in the land
of his tears,
Joseph thought
he had forgotten
the painful years.
But hearing his brother
speak love
for their aging father
and afflicted family,
Joseph began to weep
uncontrollably,
for at last
his heart did truly know
that in all the suffering
God had been in control.

May we not cry out

May we not cry out
at the sight
of the enemy,
for we know
that You
can lead us
where
You want us
to stand
and
that a barrier
at our back
can be the pressure
of Your right hand.

REFLECTION ON EXODUS 15:1-2

You provided a path

You provided a path
for Your people
through the sea,
and You will provide
a way for me
in the sea
of my tomorrow
when,
with chariots of destruction
in pursuit,
I flee to the shores
of unfailing love
and raise a tambourine
to dance
in praise of You.

Oh, Father

Oh, Father,
in the sanctuary
I see
one of your daughters,
sitting,
no longer able to stand,
and she seems
like a golden lampstand
with almond flowers
and flame
as she speaks
of Your faithful love
and glorifies
Your name.

Lord, thank you

Lord, thank you
for shortening Your stride
as You journey with me,
for otherwise
I could not accompany You,
who know
the springs of the sea
and the recesses
of the deep;
and when my eyes
begin to close
because I am weary
and need to sleep,
please carry me as I do,
wrapping me in Your peace
and holding me
close to You.

With arrows on bow strings

With arrows on bow strings,
fowlers wait in shadows
to pierce the hearts
of those who start
to wing their way
to mountains.
But safe the one
who takes refuge
in God's care
and knows to wait
for Him to break
the fowler's bow and snare.

The Lord brings me

The Lord brings me
to pasture,
verdant green,
with quiet stream
of pure,
refreshing water,
thus restoring
the downcast soul
of His feeble
yet adoring daughter.

In the valley of the shadow

In the valley
of the shadow
lurks the lion,
but in the valley
of the shadow
love endures,
for speaking
to God with us
near shadows
so unknown
makes all
within the valley
less menacing
in tone.

Plus the lion
cannot crush
the person
who by God
is shown
that into
chilling shadows
one need never
step alone,
for unto us
strength vibrating
from a
sun-emblazoned
throne.

It seemed to me

It seemed to me
her soul should be
singing in eternity
before You, Lord,
her personality
on earth
long locked
in vacancy.
Then she broke free,
eyes reaching me,
whose tears fell
relentlessly.
"I love you too,"
she said quietly,
and then I knew
how to wait
on Thee.

Lord, refine my faith

Lord,
refine
my
faith
in
Your
fire
until
in
me
You
see
Your
heart's
desire.

REFLECTION ON PSALM 91:4

I rest under His wings

I rest
under
His wings,
where
I find
Love
providing
and
perfect
peace
abiding.

I thought

I thought
my foot was slipping,
but You answered anguish
with gentle arms,
holding Your daughter tenderly,
and my joyous soul did know,
as it cast away anxiety,
that as high as the heavens
are above the earth,
so great is my Father's love
for me.

When I hear a demand

When I hear
a demand
for songs of joy,
help me lift my harp
and sing of You,
who gently took
this child's hand
and sang
through the branches
of her mind
so she could find
the blessings
which can come
when worshiping
the Holy One.

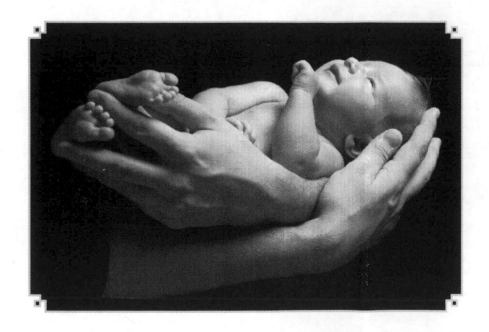

Flesh and bone

Flesh
and
bone,
woven
together
in the womb
into a body
and mind,
become
a baby
designed
to reflect
the image
of God,
who
is
Love.

Because Your thoughts

Because Your thoughts
are uncountable,
more in number
than the sand,
I can walk
on an unknown shore,
rejoicing
in the sheer immensity
of wisdom
revealed
in Your Word
to me.

Streaming upward

Streaming upward
to the mountain
of the Lord
come the nations
to adore Him
and by His light
to explore
His paths
and to find
the delight
of mankind:
the sword
become a plow.

The Lord listens

The Lord listens
for the sound
of praise,
not bangles,
and looks
for eyes
that gaze on Him,
and linen clothes
a woman wears
are nothing
to compare
with the beauty
of a woman
whose spirit is perfume.

Father

Father,
one thing
I do truly know,
and that is
the blood
of the Lamb
draws me to You,
praising
Your faithful love
and
proffering
that
Jesus, Your Son,
is my sin offering.

He spins me on His potter's wheel

He spins me
on His potter's wheel,
and so
my Father's hand I feel,
shaping me
to His design,
strengthening
this heart of mine.
Be this vessel's
dwelling place.
Fill this vessel
with your grace.
Grant it, God,
that I may be
a cup that overflows
with Thee.

Sealed alone

Sealed alone
in a den of lions
because he bowed
to God in prayer,
Daniel found
in the dark
an angel
sent by God
to deny the beasts
their bloody feast
and rescue a person
who knew
there is nothing
that God is not able to do.

You cast me into the midst

You cast me
into the midst
of swirling seas
where seaweed
wrapped around my head
and fear
began to strangle me.
Yet then,
Adonai,
I remembered You,
and my prayer rose
through the waters of the sea
and the waters of the sky
to You in the Most High,
and You spoke my salvation.

And the Word became flesh and dwelt among us, and we have seen his glory, glory as of the only Son from the Father, full of grace and truth.

John 1:14 (ESV)

REFLECTION ON LUKE 2:11-12

Salvation lying in a manger

Salvation
lying in a manger,
once wrapped in light,
now wrapped in flesh,
a stranger to sin,
yet approachable here,
and for love of us
so dependent,
this Son
from unapproachable light
resplendent.

When you know He is Lord

When you know He is Lord,
the darkest of nights
becomes Spirit bright,
and there's a star
in the east of your mind,
as you worship like shepherds
and angels of the skies,
seeing the Savior with truth-lit eyes.

REFLECTION ON MATTHEW 4:19-20

Setting down the nets

Setting down the nets
that we
have been
preparing
and
leaving
the familiar staring,
we rise
when Your call
is heard
and follow You
to a sea
where we will cast
Your Word.

Upon a foundation of rock

Upon a foundation of rock,
I built a house
which shall withstand
the rains, the winds,
and the rising streams;
and inside
my peace-filled home,
I reside
with the gentle Carpenter,
who has been, is, and will be
my Shalom.

The kingdom of heaven

The kingdom of heaven
seems
like a tiny mustard seed
planted in a field
and sending forth roots,
forerunners of change;
and
despite scorching heat
and raging winds,
with the passing
of unmarked hours,
birds nest
in its branches
and the tree flowers.

Lord, please teach us

Lord,
please
teach us
as
we
teach
children
Your Word
and
then
rejoice
to see
them
listen
to
Your voice.

Earth hosting light

Earth
hosting
light
shows
that
despite
Death's
long
night
the
Dayspring
has
risen.

Here is Jesus

Here is Jesus,
asking to enter
and eat with me
as I approach
the door to surrender,
which I open quietly
at His urging tender,
and
find myself
to be
a baby sister
of the King
in splendor,
to whom
I merely
had intended
to render
allegiance.

Jesus, with gale storm winds returning

Jesus,
with gale storm winds
returning,
I bow
for I am learning
that fear
will cause
endless churning
unless you calm
the winds
and
waves
of the sea
within me.

All my friends have faces

All my friends have faces,
except You, Jesus,
my dearest friend,
into whose eyes
one day
I shall sing
pure praise,
but until then
I gather children
in my arms,
speaking Your tender love,
and as I do,
for a moment in their eyes
I see a glimpse of You.

Weeping, she came

Weeping, she came
to Jesus,
expressing
adoration,
and
the room filled
with fragrance
and indignation
as she
displayed
love
for her Master
with a flask
of alabaster.

When my heart knew

When my heart knew
that first I must love
the Lord my God,
I did not know
my heart would break
before I could.
Nor did I understand
that Your hand
would hold the pieces
and bind up my heart anew
with comfort and with joy
in so dearly loving You.

Father, I left Your home

Father, I left Your home
for a distant country
where I squandered
all that you had given me,
and as time passed,
growing hungry
and able to see my sin,
I decided to go home again
and ask if I could be
just a hired hand.
But You,
seeing Your child of folly
from afar,
ran to meet me,
who, so unclean and so unworthy,
knew I was still your child
when unhesitatingly
You wrapped Your arms
around me.

Long ago I threw down

Long ago I threw down
my necklace of pride
at the foot of the cross
where Jesus died
and found a robe
that smelled distinctly
of forgiveness;
and wrapping myself
in this garment
much too big for me,
I found myself warm
and at peace
in its comforting fleece.

Herod arrested

Herod arrested
John the Baptist,
a voice from the desert
with an appetite
for locusts, wild honey,
and truth;
and though bound
in prison misery,
John knew
that he was free,
and that no edge
of a sword
would separate him
from the love of his Lord.

Heart clocks are set in motion

Heart clocks are set in motion
by the Almighty One,
who spins our fragile earth
around its fiery sun.
He holds His children's hearts
in His outreaching hand
that sent His only Son
to rescue godless man.
Thus, when heart clocks are stopped,
it's by Love's voice alone,
resounding through the heart:
"My child, you can come home."

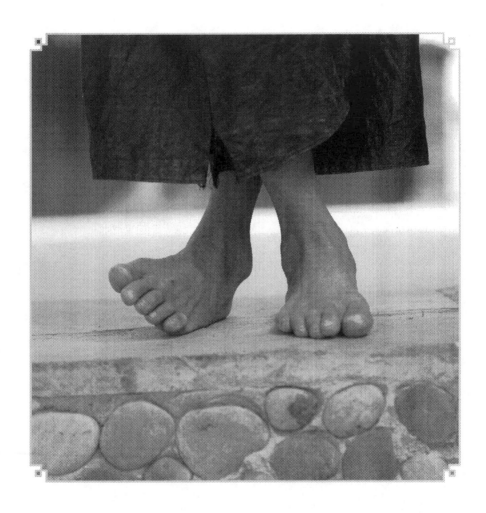

Even though my time to go

Even though
my time to go
has not yet come,
may I rise
from the evening meal,
wrap a towel
around my waist,
kneel,
and lift in my hands
the feet
of a weary woman or man;
and as I wash
my sister's or brother's feet,
may Christ's body
know His touch so sweet.

Speaking with the Lord

Speaking
with the Lord
and listening
with her heart,
a woman
of Samaria
drank
with elation
the water
of life
at the well
of salvation.

REFLECTION ON JOHN 20:26-29

Jesus, I will never ask

Jesus, I will never ask
to see the nail marks
in Your hands,
for my life's cry will be
that You reached out
and touched this child
who looked to You expectantly,
and by Your mighty hand
I have been made whole,
no longer lost and affrighted,
but wholly Yours,
and in You,
my Lord and my God,
wholly delighted.

Rejoice

Rejoice,
for now
grafted
are we,
olive branches,
a holy tree,
because
the Son
laid
down
His life
for
us
on a cross
at Calvary.

From our minds

From our minds
may Your Word
pour
so that
those who pant
for You
on burning sands
may drink
of You
and thirst no more.

You helped me

You helped me
to pick up my shield
when flaming arrows
began to fall,
and as a wind
gently blew out
the arrows of fear,
I felt you near.
Then it was later,
quiet in Your love,
that I heard
Your Word:
"Love never ends."

Transplanted am I

Transplanted am I,
now rooted
in God's love,
bearing fruit,
strengthened
by His might,
and
receiving
an inheritance
in His
glorious kingdom
of light.

Housed are we in tents

Housed are we in tents
that the storms of time
will tear,
and though we long
to live elsewhere,
we wait with confidence,
for His Spirit dwells
within our tents
until they fold
and we enter
our new residence
divinely clothed.

You wielded Your Word

You wielded Your Word,
sharper than a two-edged sword,
and pierced my heart,
passing through the chambers,
marking and then slashing down
unclean thoughts
and attitudes
You found;
and having put me to the sword,
You did not depart,
but loving me,
You left Your sword
living in my heart.

My heart having been set free

My heart having been set free,
I run the race
marked out for me,
throwing off
entangling sin
as I race toward Him,
who, for joy,
ran the race of man,
and endured the cross
steadfastly
so that now,
sitting at God's right hand,
He might champion me.

At God's command

At God's command
to leave comfort
and travel
to a distant land,
we can only go,
even if
we do not know
where we will pitch
our tent;
and it is
in that land
that we are meant
to live by faith
amidst adversity,
knowing
God's promises
will be fulfilled
in time
and
in eternity.

Hold me fast

Hold me fast
in Your
refining fire
until my faith,
more precious
than liquid gold,
pours out
before You,
the King,
as a love offering
of molten praise.

Suddenly surprised by joy

Suddenly
surprised
by
joy,
I know
that
there
has come
a reminder
from the Holy One
of His Presence
though unseen.

In Him we walk

In Him we walk,
with His love in us,
and our steps are the same,
taking us
on stony paths
because we bear His name,
leading into pressing crowds
and into the marketplace,
where we will hear
the enemy's voice
or
see the enemy's face;
and then
we must remember
Christ chose the path
to Calvary,
even as in our own lives,
because we love
must we.

REFLECTION ON 1 JOHN 2:8

With the darkness passing

With the darkness passing,
help me to bind
every thought
for You
so that
my mind can bow
to Your commands
and
my heart can rise
in delight
as I stand and love
my brothers and sisters
with whom I live
in shining light.

Hate winding like a snake

Hate winding like a snake
strikes the one
who forsakes
the command
to love his brother,
and in darkness blinding
he stumbles finding
the cost to be
the fangs of hate
upon his soul.

I collected the world within

I collected the world within,
yet You cleansed my heart
and brought in Your wisdom,
wherein came desire
for that which moth and rust
cannot destroy
and which no thief can steal.
You filled me
so I might do Your will
and be Your friend
in a world
which does not comprehend
that a heart can yearn to hold
only Heaven's gold.

Somewhere near the cross

Somewhere near
the cross
I saw
You loved me.
I had stumbled there
unaware,
though now I see
You cleared
my footpath
silently
so that I might find
when my heart called
You would answer
and envelop me
in waves of love
from eternity.

May these words be pleasing

May these words be pleasing
in Your sight, dear Lord,
as You watch them travel
to a stranger or friend,
and when others
meet these words,
may they be encouraged
to spend
"a few handbreadths"* of days
sending forth
their own words of praise.

* handbreadth: the width of a palm or 4 fingers

Let the words of my mouth
and the meditation of
my heart
be acceptable in your sight,
O Lord, my rock and my
redeemer.

Psalm 19:14 (ESV)

Printed in the United States
By Bookmasters